D1447074

Talking Service

Readings for Civic Reflection

Edited by Adam Davis and Elizabeth Lynn

Published and distributed by

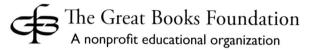

The Great Books Foundation
A nonprofit educational organization

35 E. Wacker Drive, Suite 400
Chicago, IL 60601
www.greatbooks.org

ISBN 978-1-880323-74-8

First printing
9 8 7 6 5 4 3 2 1

Library of Congress Cataloging-in-Publication Data

Talking service : readings for civic reflection / edited by Adam Davis and
Elizabeth Lynn.
     p. cm.
"This booklet was adapted from The civically engaged reader : a diverse collec-
tion of short provocative readings on civic activity"--T.p. verso.

ISBN 978-1-880323-74-8 (alk. paper)
1. Civics. 2. Political participation. I. Project on Civic Reflection. II. Civically
engaged reader.

JF801.T25 2008
323.6'5--dc22
                                        2008030411

Contents

Why Talk Service?

Today in the United States, hundreds of thousands of people are getting involved in volunteering. High school students participate in service learning programs; young adults follow up high school or college with a year of service; and older adults sign up to volunteer through their community service center, workplace, or house of worship. They join with local or national organizations that put them to work in areas where urgent help is needed: schools, hospitals, disaster-stricken neighborhoods—wherever a set of hands can make a difference.

Yet anyone who serves—from the seasoned relief worker to the first-time volunteer—knows that it is not always clear *what* difference is being made. Service experiences are not only urgent but also complicated. Yes, service helps to accomplish important work, but it also raises unsettling questions:

- Is it right for me to expect certain things from the people I am trying to help?
- Why am I serving *these* people—and not the many others in need?
- Am I changing the world by serving, or am I keeping it from changing?
- Is service changing me?

These questions are large, complex, and worthwhile, but they often get lost or put aside while we hustle to get things done. Reflection sounds beneficial, but it is hard to carve out time for reflection, and it is harder still to make it happen in a way that is meaningful and enjoyable.

Yet if we do not find time to reflect on our service, we run the risk of losing touch with the reasons we serve in the first place. And if we do not find ways to reflect both together and more deeply on our service, we run the risk of losing our connection to one another and to the larger community we help to build.

One way to help service volunteers reflect more deeply on their experience is to bring them together regularly to discuss short readings that raise basic questions about civic activity —texts such as those found in *Talking Service*. We call this practice *civic reflection*.

As a practice, civic reflection is fairly straightforward and low tech. A group of volunteers gathers for an hour or so to talk about a short story, or a poem, or a memoir. Perhaps they share food or meet in a classroom or at the service site itself. A facilitator leads them in the conversation, asking specific questions about the reading that gradually open onto larger questions about their own civic choices and experiences. This discussion may be designed as a special stand-alone event, or it may be built into the ongoing activities of the group—as part of a training day, orientation session, staff meeting, or retreat or during class time.

As simple as the process sounds, civic reflection can have wonderfully enriching results: it can both challenge and deepen civic engagement as participants begin to think and talk with one another about the assumptions and beliefs that underlie their activity. The result, as one participant has observed, is "a resource from which I can draw greater perspective in delivering service."

How to Use This Book

Talking Service contains seven readings chosen to spur reflection on the experience of service. Each is short enough to read on the spot, yet complex enough to provoke discussion. These readings may be approached in any order.

We chose these particular readings for *Talking Service* because they raise basic but profound questions about the experience of service. They do not answer these central questions, nor do they tell us what to think or how to feel about our service. Instead, they invite us to ask ourselves what *we* really think about our experience as volunteers. They are more provocative than inspirational—not necessarily bulletin-board material, but the kind of reading that gets us thinking and makes us want to hear what others think, too.

The book provides two kinds of questions after every reading:

1. An opening reflection exercise, which participants can complete silently, use as a writing assignment, or discuss in pairs. We recommend allotting five to ten minutes for the reflection exercise.

2. A set of questions for group discussion. In general, these questions begin with the reading itself and then move toward making connections between the reading and participants' own service experiences. The group does not need to take up all these questions or take them up in the order presented. A few of these questions, thoughtfully pursued, may be enough for a single conversation.

Finally, we recommend reading the selection aloud between the opening reflection exercise and the group discussion when possible. We also advise setting aside a few minutes at the end of the discussion for individual reflection or evaluation.

We hope that this little book will serve those who serve others by making it easier to talk about, as well as carry out, the extraordinary work of service.

Adam Davis and Elizabeth Lynn
Editors, *Talking Service*

Bertolt Brecht
A Bed for the Night

I hear that in New York
At the corner of 26th Street and Broadway
A man stands every evening during the winter months
And gets beds for the homeless there
By appealing to passers-by.

It won't change the world
It won't improve relations among men
It will not shorten the age of exploitation
But a few men have a bed for the night
For a night the wind is kept from them
The snow meant for them falls on the roadway.

Don't put down the book on reading this, man.

A few people have a bed for the night
For a night the wind is kept from them
The snow meant for them falls on the roadway
But it won't change the world
It won't improve relations among men
It will not shorten the age of exploitation.

Questions for "A Bed for the Night"

For Reflection

Take a few moments to think about an individual who has made meaningful social change. How did you hear about this person? What strikes you as meaningful about what this person is doing or has done?

For Group Discussion

Why does the poem start where it starts?

Why does the narrator begin by telling us that what he is going to describe is hearsay? Why is he so specific about the location?

Why does the man in the poem ask for help for the homeless by standing outside in the winter weather? What exactly is the man asking for?

Why does the narrator make a point of telling us that the man's action "won't change the world / It won't improve relations among men / It will not shorten the age of exploitation"?

In speaking of the men who have a bed for the night, why does the narrator say that the snow is "meant for them"?

In the middle of the poem, why does the narrator emphasize that the reader is holding a book? Why does the narrator tell the reader *not* to put down the book?

Why, after telling the reader not to put down the book, does the narrator proceed to repeat the previous six lines with slight variations?

Is the kind of service you provide changing the world? Is service in general about changing the world?

Pablo Neruda
The Lamb and the Pinecone

One time, investigating in the backyard of our house in Temuco the tiny objects and minuscule beings of my world, I came upon a hole in one of the boards of the fence. I looked through the hole and saw a landscape like that behind our house, uncared for and wild. I moved back a few steps, because I sensed vaguely that something was about to happen. All of a sudden a hand appeared—a tiny hand of a boy about my own age. By the time I came close again, the hand was gone, and in its place there was a marvelous white sheep.

The sheep's wool was faded. Its wheels had escaped. All of this only made it more authentic. I had never seen such a wonderful sheep. I looked back through the hole but the boy had disappeared. I went into the house and brought out a treasure of my own: a pinecone, opened, full of odor and resin, which I adored. I set it down in the same spot and went off with the sheep.

I never saw either the hand or the boy again. And I have never again seen a sheep like that either. The toy I lost finally in a fire. But even now, in 1954, almost fifty years old, whenever I pass a toy shop, I look furtively into the window, but it's no use. They don't make sheep like that anymore.

I have been a lucky man. To feel the intimacy of brothers is a marvelous thing in life. To feel the love of people whom we love is a fire that feeds our life. But to feel the affection that comes from those whom we do not know, from those unknown to us, who are watching over our sleep and solitude, over our dangers and our weaknesses—that is something still greater and more beautiful because it widens out the boundaries of our being and unites all living things.

That exchange brought home to me for the first time a precious idea: that all of humanity is somehow together. That experience came to me again much later; this time it stood out strikingly against a background of trouble and persecution.

It won't surprise you then that I attempted to give something resiny, earthlike, and fragrant in exchange for human brotherhood. Just as I once left the pinecone by the fence, I have since left my words on the door of so many people who were unknown to me, people in prison, or hunted, or alone.

That is the great lesson I learned in my childhood, in the backyard of a lonely house. Maybe it was nothing but a game two boys played who didn't know each other and wanted to pass to the other some good things of life. Yet maybe this small and mysterious exchange of gifts remained inside me also, deep and indestructible, giving my poetry light.

Questions for "The Lamb and the Pinecone"

For Reflection

What is the most meaningful gift you have ever received? What is the most meaningful gift you have ever given?

For Group Discussion

Why does the boy on the other side of the fence leave the sheep? Why does he disappear after leaving it?

Why does Neruda leave his pinecone for the boy?

What does Neruda mean when he talks about a widening of the "boundaries of our being"?

How does the exchange of the sheep and the pinecone bring home to Neruda that "all of humanity is somehow together"?

Why does Neruda call this exchange of gifts "mysterious"?

For something to be a gift, does there have to be an exchange of some kind?

Langston Hughes
Theme for English B

The instructor said,

>*Go home and write*
>*a page tonight.*
>*And let that page come out of you—*
>*Then, it will be true.*

I wonder if it's that simple?
I am twenty-two, colored, born in Winston-Salem.
I went to school there, then Durham, then here
to this college on the hill above Harlem.
I am the only colored student in my class.
The steps from the hill lead down into Harlem,
through a park, then I cross St. Nicholas,
Eighth Avenue, Seventh, and I come to the Y,
the Harlem Branch Y, where I take the elevator
up to my room, sit down, and write this page:

It's not easy to know what is true for you or me
at twenty-two, my age. But I guess I'm what
I feel and see and hear, Harlem, I hear you:
hear you, hear me—we two—you, me, talk on this page.
(I hear New York, too.) Me—who?
Well, I like to eat, sleep, drink, and be in love.
I like to work, read, learn, and understand life.

I like a pipe for a Christmas present,
or records—Bessie, bop, or Bach.
I guess being colored doesn't make me *not* like
the same things other folks like who are other races.
So will my page be colored that I write?

Being me, it will not be white.
But it will be
a part of you, instructor.
You are white—
yet a part of me, as I am a part of you.
That's American.
Sometimes perhaps you don't want to be a part of me.
Nor do I often want to be a part of you.
But we are, that's true!
As I learn from you,
I guess you learn from me—
although you're older—and white—
and somewhat more free.

This is my page for English B.

Questions for
"Theme for English B"

For Reflection

Think of an instance when someone you were talking to "got you wrong" in some way or made a mistaken assumption about who you were. How did you recognize and react to this? Were you able to overcome your sense that this person had gotten you wrong? If so, how?

For Group Discussion

What is the purpose of the teacher's assignment?

Why does the assignment begin with the words, "Go home"?

Why does the narrator respond to the assignment by thinking of differences?

What separates the narrator from his classmates and his teacher? What unifies them?

What does the narrator mean by "will my page be colored that I write?" Will it?

What kind of relationship does the poet want with his instructor? Does his "Theme" help achieve it?

How important is it to connect across differences? How possible is it?

Jean-Jacques Rousseau
Selection from

Reveries of the Solitary Walker

At a corner of the boulevard near the Enfer toll gate exit, there is a woman who sets up a stand every day in the summer to sell fruit, herb tea, and rolls. This woman has a very nice, but lame, little boy who, hobbling along on his crutches, goes about quite graciously asking passersby for alms. I had become slightly acquainted with this little fellow; each time I passed, he did not fail to come pay his little compliment, always followed by my little offering. At first I was charmed to see him; I gave to him very goodheartedly and for some time continued to do so with the same pleasure, quite frequently even prompting and listening to his little prattle, which I found enjoyable. This pleasure, having gradually become a habit, was inexplicably transformed into a kind of duty I soon felt to be annoying, especially because of the preliminary harangue to which I had to listen and in which he never failed to call me Monsieur Rousseau many times, to show that he knew me well. But to the contrary, that only taught me that he knew me no more than those who had instructed him. From that time on I passed by there less willingly, and finally I automatically got in the habit of making a detour when I came close to this crossing. . . .

. . . I have often felt the burden of my own good deeds by the chain of duties they later entailed. Then the pleasure disappeared, and the continuation of the very attentiveness that had charmed me at first no longer struck me as anything but an almost unbearable annoyance. During my brief moments of prosperity, many people appealed to me; and despite the multitude of favors they asked of me, none of them was ever turned away. But from these first good deeds, which my heart poured out effusively, were forged chains of subsequent liabilities I had not foreseen and whose yoke I could no longer shake off. In the eyes of those who received them, my first favors were only a pledge for those that were supposed to follow; and as soon as some unfortunate man had hooked me with my own good deed, that was it from then on. This first free and voluntary good deed became an unlimited right to all those he might need afterward, without even my lack of power being enough to release me from his claim. That is how very delightful enjoyments were transformed into onerous subjections for me ever afterward.

I know that there is a kind of contract, and even the holiest of all, between the benefactor and the beneficiary. They form a sort of society with each other, more restricted than the one that unites men in general. And if the beneficiary tacitly pledges himself to gratitude, the benefactor likewise pledges himself to preserve for the other, as long as he does not make himself unworthy of it, the same goodwill he has just shown him and to renew its acts for him whenever he is able to and whenever it is required. Those are not stated conditions, but they are natural effects of the relationship that has just been set up between them. He who refuses a spontaneous favor the first time it is asked of him gives the one he has refused no right to complain. But he who, in a similar case, refuses the same person the same kindness he heretofore accorded him, frustrates a hope he has authorized him to conceive. He deceives and belies an expectation he has engendered. In this refusal, we feel an inexplicable injustice and greater harshness than in the other; but it is no less the effect of an independence the heart loves and renounces only with effort. When I pay a debt, it is a duty I fulfill; when I give a gift, it is a pleasure I give myself. Now, the pleasure of fulfilling our duties is one of those that only the habit of virtue engenders; those that come to us immediately from nature do not rise so high.

Questions for
"Reveries of the Solitary Walker"

For Reflection

Have you ever stopped helping someone whom you had been helping? What caused you to stop? What might have kept you from stopping?

For Group Discussion

Why does Rousseau give money to the crippled boy? Why does doing so give Rousseau pleasure?

Why is the boy asking for alms?

Why is Rousseau disturbed by the boy's familiar attitude in addressing him as Monsieur Rousseau? Why does this lead Rousseau to avoid the boy?

How, according to Rousseau, can giving start out as a pleasant experience and then become unpleasant and onerous, or burdensome?

According to Rousseau, how is the contract between giver and receiver, benefactor and beneficiary, "the holiest of all"?

What does Rousseau mean when he says that the pleasures that "come to us immediately from nature do not rise so high" as those that come from fulfilling our duties?

Having helped someone once, do we have a responsibility to continue helping that person? When is it right to stop helping the person?

Franz Kafka
Fellowship

We are five friends; one day we came out of a house one after the other; first one came and placed himself beside the gate, then the second came, or rather he glided through the gate like a little ball of quicksilver, and placed himself near the first one, then came the third, then the fourth, then the fifth. Finally we all stood in a row. People began to notice us; they pointed at us and said: those five just came out of that house. Since then we have been living together; it would be a peaceful life if it weren't for a sixth one continually trying to interfere. He doesn't do us any harm, but he annoys us, and that is harm enough; why does he intrude where he is not wanted? We don't know him and don't want him to join us. There was a time, of course, when the five of us did not know one another, either; and it could be said that we still don't know one another, but what is possible and can be tolerated by the five of us is not possible and cannot be tolerated with this sixth one. In any case, we are five and don't want to be six. And what is the point of this continual being together anyhow? It is also pointless for the five of us, but here we are together and will remain together; a new combination, however, we do not want, just because of our experiences. But how is one to make all this clear to the sixth one? Long explanations would almost amount to accepting him in our circle, so we prefer not to explain and not to accept him. No matter how he pouts his lips we push him away with our elbows, but however much we push him away, back he comes.

Questions for "Fellowship"

For Reflection

Consider a group that you "belong" to—what allows you to be a part of the group? Consider a group you don't belong to—why aren't you a part of that group?

For Group Discussion

Why does the narrator say that he and the other four are "friends"? Why do they continue to associate with one another?

How is the sixth one annoying to the first five? Why don't they "want to be six"?

Is there anything that the first five would need to know about the sixth for him to join them?

Why is the narrator skeptical about "long explanations"?

Why does the sixth keep coming back?

Why do you think Kafka titled this piece "Fellowship"?

Where does fellowship come from, and what sustains it?

Is a feeling of fellowship part of your service experience? With whom do you feel that fellowship?

Jane Addams
Earliest Impressions

On the theory that our genuine impulses may be connected with our childish experiences, that one's bent may be tracked back to that "No-Man's Land" where character is formless but nevertheless settling into definite lines of future development, I begin this record with some impressions of my childhood. . . .

I recall an incident which must have occurred before I was seven years old, for the mill in which my father transacted his business that day was closed in 1867. The mill stood in the neighboring town adjacent to its poorest quarter. Before then I had always seen the little city of ten thousand people with the admiring eyes of a country child, and it had never occurred to me that all its streets were not as bewilderingly attractive as the one which contained the glittering toyshop and the confectioner. On that day I had my first sight of the poverty which implies squalor, and felt the curious distinction between the ruddy poverty of the country and that which even a small city presents in its shabbiest streets. I remember launching at my father the pertinent inquiry why people lived in such horrid little houses so close together, and that after receiving his explanation I declared with much firmness when I grew up I should, of course, have a large house, but it would not be built among the other large houses, but right in the midst of horrid little houses like these. . . .

Although I constantly confided my sins and perplexities to my father, there are only a few occasions on which I remember having received direct advice or admonition; it may easily be true, however, that I have forgotten the latter, in the manner of many seekers after advice who enjoyably set forth their situation but do not really listen to the advice itself. I can remember an admonition on one occasion, however, when, as a little girl of eight years, arrayed in a new cloak, gorgeous beyond anything I had ever worn before, I stood before my father for his approval. I was much chagrined by his remark that it was a very pretty cloak—in fact so much prettier than any cloak the other little girls in the Sunday School had, that he would advise me to wear my old cloak, which would keep me quite as warm, with the added advantage of not making the other little girls feel bad. I complied with the request but I fear without inner consent, and I certainly was quite without the joy of self-sacrifice as I walked soberly through the village street by the side of my counselor. My mind was busy, however, with the old question eternally suggested by the inequalities of the human lot. Only as we neared the church door did I venture to ask what could be done about it, receiving the reply that it might never be righted so far as clothes went, but that people might be equal in things that mattered much more than clothes, the affairs of education and religion, for instance, which we attended to when we went to school and church, and that it was very stupid to wear the sort of clothes that made it harder to have equality even there.

Questions for "Earliest Impressions"

For Reflection

If you look back on your own childhood, what are some of your own earliest impressions of inequality? How did you respond? How did the adults who were close to you encourage you to respond?

For Group Discussion

Why does Addams offer an account of her earliest impressions? How can recalling early childhood impressions give insight into our impulses now?

What do you think Addams's father says to her about the different neighborhoods in her community? What is your explanation of these differences?

Why does Addams want to live in a large house among the small houses?

Why does Addams's father discourage Addams from wearing her cloak to church? Do you agree with him?

What does Addams mean by the "old question eternally suggested by the inequalities of the human lot?" How would you respond to this question?

Are there connections between your own earliest impressions and your impulse to serve—or not to serve—others?

Martin Luther King Jr.
A Gift of Love

This Christmas I remember the little black children of Grenada, Mississippi, beaten by grown men as they walked to school. I remember a baby, attacked by rats in a Chicago slum. I remember a young Negro, murdered by a gang in Cicero, Illinois, where he was looking for a job; and a white minister in Georgia, forced out of his sacred office because he spoke for human dignity. I remember, too, farm workers in Mississippi, risking their lives and their livelihood to march out of the cotton fields and vote for freedom and democracy.

This I remember, especially in this season of giving, for thes people have followed the example and spirit of Christ himself. They have given mankind a priceless "Gift of Love."

I am thinking now of some teenage boys in Chicago. They have nicknames like "Tex," and "Pueblo," and "Goat," and "Teddy." They hail from the Negro slums. Forsaken by society, they once proudly fought and lived for street gangs like the Vice Lords, the Roman Saints, the Rangers.

But this year, they gave us all the gift of nonviolence, which is indeed a gift of love.

I met these boys and heard their stories in discussions we had on some long, cold nights last winter in the slum apartment I rent in the West Side ghetto of Chicago. I was shocked at the venom they poured out against the world. At times I shared their despair and felt a hopelessness that these young Americans could ever embrace the concept of nonviolence as the effective and powerful instrument of social reform.

All their lives, boys like this have known life as a madhouse of violence and degradation. Some have never experienced a meaningful family life. Some have police records. Some dropped out of the incredibly bad slum schools, then were deprived of honorable work, then took to the streets.

To the young victim of the slums, this society has so limited the alternatives of his life that the expression of his manhood is reduced to the ability to defend himself physically. No wonder it appears logical to him to strike out, resorting to violence against oppression. That is the only way he thinks he can get recognition.

And so, we have seen occasional rioting—and, much more frequently and consistently, brutal acts and crimes by Negroes against Negroes. In many a week in Chicago, as many or more Negro youngsters have been killed in gang fights as were killed in the riots there last summer.

The Freedom Movement has tried to bring a message to boys like Tex. First, we explained that violence can be put down by armed might and police work, that physical force can never solve the underlying social problems. Second, we promised them we could prove, by example, that nonviolence works.

The young slum dweller has good reason to be suspicious of promises. But these young people in Chicago agreed last winter to give nonviolence a test. Then came the very long, very tense, hot summer of 1966, and the first test for many Chicago youngsters: the Freedom March through Mississippi. Gang members went there in carloads.

Those of us who had been in the movement for years were apprehensive about the behavior of the boys. Before the march ended, they were to be attacked by tear gas. They were to be called upon to protect women and children on the march, with no other weapon than their own bodies. To them, it would be a strange and possibly nonsensical way to respond to violence.

But they reacted splendidly! They learned in Mississippi, and returned to teach in Chicago, the beautiful lesson of acting against evil by renouncing force.

And in Chicago, the test was sterner. These marchers endured not only the filthiest kind of verbal abuse, but also barrages of rocks and sticks and eggs and cherry bombs. They did not reply in words or violent deeds. Once again, their only weapon was their own bodies. I saw boys like Goat leap into the air to catch with their bare hands the bricks and bottles that were sailed toward us.

It was through the Chicago marches that our promise to them—that nonviolence achieves results—was redeemed, and their hopes for a better life were rekindled. For they saw, in Chicago, that a humane police force—in contrast to police in Mississippi—could defend the exercise of constitutional rights as well as enforce the law in the ghetto.

They saw, in prosperous white American communities, that hatred and bigotry could and should be confronted, exposed, and dealt with. They saw, in the very heart of a great city, that men of power could be made to listen to the tramp of marching feet and the call for freedom and justice, and use their power to work for a truly Open City for all.

Boys like Teddy, a child of the slums, saw all this because they decided to rise above the cruelties of those slums and to work and march, peacefully, for human dignity. They revitalized my own faith in nonviolence. And these poverty-stricken boys enriched us all with a gift of love.

Questions for "A Gift of Love"

For Reflection

Think of someone who has given a gift to humanity. What was the gift? How was it given? In what sense was it a gift to humanity rather than to specific human beings?

For Group Discussion

What do the people King remembers in the first paragraph have in common?

Why does the "young victim of the slums" King talks about want to "get recognition"? What does King mean when he says, "No wonder it appears logical to him to strike out"?

Why do you think King gives (and uses) specific names like Teddy and Tex in this piece?

What is the "truly Open City for all" that King mentions in the second-to-last paragraph?

In what sense are the actions of Teddy and the other boys "a gift of love"? What is the content of the gift, and to whom is it given?

Does King himself give any gifts over the course of the events described here? How do these gifts come to be recognized or accepted, if at all?

About the Authors

Bertolt Brecht (1898–1956) was born into a prosperous and pious middle-class family in Augsburg, Germany. As a young man, he began medical studies in Munich but abandoned them to become a poet and playwright. His first play, *Baal*, was produced in 1923; *The Threepenny Opera* followed in 1928. A communist and advocate of social reform, Brecht saw his plays and other writings banned in Germany in the 1930s. He went into exile in 1933, living first in Scandinavia and then the United States, where he wrote briefly and without much success for Hollywood. Upon his return to Germany in 1948, Brecht became that country's most popular contemporary poet, finding an audience on both sides of the political divide. His poem "A Bed for the Night" appeared in his *Collected Poems 1913–1956*.

Pablo Neruda (1904–1973) was born Neftalí Ricardo Reyes Basoalto in Parral, Chile. When he was thirteen, he contributed a few articles and his first published poem to *El Mañana*. In 1920, he contributed to the literary journal *Selva Austral* under the name Pablo Neruda, which he adopted in memory of the Czech poet Jan Neruda. From the late 1920s on, Neruda traveled extensively and became active in political causes. He published many books of poetry, as well as memoirs and prose. Neruda received the Nobel Prize in Literature in 1971 and died in 1973. "The Lamb and the Pinecone" comes from an interview with Robert Bly, which first appeared in a volume edited by Bly, *Vallejo and Neruda: Selected Poems*.

Langston Hughes (1902–1967) was born in Joplin, Missouri, and grew up in Lawrence, Kansas, and Cleveland, Ohio. By the time he entered Columbia University in 1921, Hughes had begun to make a name for himself as a poet. After leaving

Columbia to work on ships and his writing, Hughes graduated from Lincoln University in Pennsylvania. He became one of the leading figures in the Harlem Renaissance and in the African American literary tradition more generally, publishing fiction, drama, journalism, autobiography, translation, and poetry. "Theme for English B" was first published in 1951.

Jean-Jacques Rousseau (1712–1778), the son of a Swiss watchmaker, became a central figure of the French Enlightenment and inspired political revolutionaries on two continents. He wrote what has come to be classified as political theory and anthropology, as well as a wildly successful novel, a powerful treatise on education, and one of the first modern autobiographies. As a young man, Rousseau roamed around Europe, attempting various failed routes to fame and fortune (including the invention of a new system of musical notation). As an older man, in addition to publishing several influential books, Rousseau copied music and devoted much of his energy to botany. The selection comes from his last work, *The Reveries of the Solitary Walker*, published four years after his death.

Franz Kafka (1883–1924) was born in the Jewish ghetto of Prague. He earned a law degree and became a clerk for an accident insurance company. Though Kafka wrote a number of compelling stories and novels, he published little during his lifetime. As he was dying of tuberculosis, Kafka requested that his unpublished manuscripts be burned. However, his good friend Max Brod preserved them, including "A Hunger Artist," *The Castle*, and *The Trial*. "Fellowship," translated by Tania and James Stern, was written between 1917 and 1923.

Jane Addams (1860–1935) was born in Cedarville, Illinois. As a young woman she founded Hull House, a residential community that offered a wide range of help and hospitality to immigrants on Chicago's West Side. Addams lived and worked at Hull House for the rest of her life while also writing and speaking on an ever-widening stage. Her efforts on behalf of international peace earned her the Nobel Peace Prize in 1931. "Earliest Impressions" is from the opening chapter of her memoir, *Twenty Years at Hull-House.*

Martin Luther King Jr. (1929–1968), the leading figure of the civil rights movement in America, is revered around the world as a martyr for racial equality, social justice, and nonviolence. Born in Atlanta, King enrolled at Morehouse College at the age of fifteen. Four years later, he had completed his degree and was ordained a Baptist minister. He later received a PhD in systematic theology from Boston University. In 1964, King was awarded the Nobel Peace Prize. He was assassinated in Memphis, Tennessee, four years later.

Acknowledgments

All possible care has been taken to trace ownership and to secure permission for each selection in this anthology. The Great Books Foundation thanks the following authors, publishers, and representatives for permission to reprint copyrighted material:

A Bed for the Night, by Bertolt Brecht, translated by Georg Rapp, from BERTOLT BRECHT: POEMS 1913–1956, translated by John Willet and Ralph Manheim. Copyright © 1976, 1979 by Methuen London. Reprinted by permission of the Taylor & Francis Group, LLC, a division of Informa plc.

The Lamb and the Pinecone, by Pablo Neruda, from NERUDA AND VALLEJO: SELECTED POEMS, edited by Robert Bly. Copyright © 1976 by Robert Bly. Reprinted by permission of Robert Bly.

Theme for English B, by Langston Hughes, from THE COLLECTED POEMS OF LANGSTON HUGHES by Langston Hughes, edited by Arnold Rampersad with David Roessel, Associate Editor, copyright © 1994 by the Estate of Langston Hughes. Used by permission of Alfred A. Knopf, a division of Random House, Inc.

Selection from THE REVERIES OF THE SOLITARY WALKER, by Jean-Jacques Rousseau, translated by Charles E. Butterworth. Copyright © 1992 by Hackett Publishing Company, Inc. Reprinted by permission of Hackett Publishing Company, Inc. All rights reserved.

Fellowship, by Franz Kafka, edited by Nahum N. Glatzer, translated by Tania and James Stern, from FRANZ KAFKA: THE COMPLETE STORIES by Franz Kafka, edited by Nahum N. Glatzer, copyright © 1946, 1947, 1948, 1949, 1954, 1958, 1971 by Schocken Books. Used by permission of Schoken Books, a division of Random House, Inc.

Earliest Impressions, from TWENTY YEARS AT HULL-HOUSE, by Jane Addams, copyright © 1961 by Henry Steele Commager. Reprinted by permission of Signet, an imprint of Penguin Group (USA) Inc.

A Gift of Love, by Martin Luther King Jr, from A TESTAMENT OF HOPE: THE ESSENTIAL WRITINGS AND SPEECHES OF MARTIN LUTHER KING JR., copyright © 1958 by Martin Luther King, copyright © renewed 1986 by Coretta Scott King. Reprinted by arrangement with Writer's House LLC, New York City.